1 How ma

 +  **=**

A ● 3   C ● 2

B ● 4   D ● 5

2 How many in all?

 **=**

A ● 4   C ● 5

B ● 7   D ● 6

How many in all?

+ **=**

A ⬤ 8   C ⬤ 5

B ⬤ 9   D ⬤ 6

How many in all?

+ **=**

A ⬤ 6   C ⬤ 9

B ⬤ 7   D ⬤ 4

5. How many in all?

$+$ $=$

A ⬤ 11   C ⬤ 10

B ⬤ 8   D ⬤ 9

6. How many in all?

$+$ $=$

A ⬤ 9   C ⬤ 12

B ⬤ 10   D ⬤ 8

How many in all?

A ● 13   C ● 12

B ● 9   D ● 11

How many in all?

A ● 15   C ● 13

B ● 14   D ● 12

9 How many in all?

A ● 13   C ● 14

B ● 16   D ● 15

10 How many in all?

A ● 19   C ● 18

B ● 15   D ● 17

How many in all?

 + =

A ● 15   C ● 14

B ● 18   D ● 17

How many in all?

 + =

A ● 20   C ● 19

B ● 10   D ● 0

13

Solve the problem.

$$3 + 1$$

A ● 3

B ● 4

C ● 2

D ● 5

14

Solve the problem.

$$4 + 2 = \underline{\quad}$$

A ● 6   C ● 4

B ● 7   D ● 5

Solve the problem.

$$6 + 3 = \rule{2cm}{0.4pt}$$

A ● 7   C ● 8

B ● 10   D ● 9

Solve the problem.

$$\begin{array}{r} 3 \\ + 8 \\ \hline \end{array}$$

A ● 13

B ● 11

C ● 12

D ● 10

17 Solve the problem.

$$\begin{array}{r} 2 \\ +\ 5 \\ \hline \end{array}$$

A ● 9

B ● 7

C ● 10

D ● 8

18 Solve the problem.

$$5 + 4 = \underline{\hspace{1cm}}$$

A ● 12   C ● 9

B ● 11   D ● 10

19 Solve the problem.

$$4 + 7 = \underline{\hspace{2cm}}$$

A ● 11   C ● 9

B ● 13   D ● 12

20 Solve the problem.

$$\begin{array}{r} 9 \\ + 2 \\ \hline \end{array}$$

A ● 8

B ● 12

C ● 10

D ● 11

21

Solve the problem.

$$8 + 5$$

A ● 14

B ● 11

C ● 13

D ● 12

22

Solve the problem.

$$7 + 7 = \underline{}$$

A ● 14   C ● 16

B ● 15   D ● 13

23

Solve the problem.

$$10 + 4 = \underline{\hspace{2cm}}$$

A ⬤ 13   C ⬤ 24

B ⬤ 6   D ⬤ 14

24

Solve the problem.

$$\begin{array}{r} 11 \\ +\ 6 \\ \hline \end{array}$$

A ⬤ 17

B ⬤ 19

C ⬤ 18

D ⬤ 16

25

Solve the problem.

$$14 + 3$$

A ● 16
B ● 17
C ● 18
D ● 15

26

Solve the problem.

$$12 + 7 = \_\_\_$$

A ● 17   C ● 19
B ● 21   D ● 20

Solve the problem.

15 + 3 = ___

A ● 18   C ● 19

B ● 17   D ● 20

28

Solve the problem.

$$18 \\ + \; 2$$

A ● 21

B ● 18

C ● 19

D ● 20

29 Provide the missing number.

$$4 + \square = 5$$

A ⬤ 0

B ⬤ 2

C ⬤ 1

D ⬤ 3

30 Provide the missing number.

$$2 + \square = 4$$

A ⬤ 1   C ⬤ 3

B ⬤ 2   D ⬤ 0

31

Provide the missing number.

$$\square + 3 = 7$$

A ● 4   C ● 5

B ● 3   D ● 2

32

Provide the missing number.

$$\begin{array}{r} \square \\ + \ 2 \\ \hline 6 \end{array}$$

A ● 3

B ● 5

C ● 4

D ● 6

33 Provide the missing number.

$$5 + \square = 10$$

A ● 4

B ● 6

C ● 2

D ● 5

34 Provide the missing number.

$$\square + 7 = 11$$

A ● 4

B ● 2

C ● 5

D ● 3

Provide the missing number.

$$\boxed{} + 5 = 15$$

A ● 11   C ● 9

B ● 10   D ● 8

36

Provide the missing number.

$$\begin{array}{r} \boxed{} \\ + 6 \\ \hline 19 \end{array}$$

A ● 13

B ● 15

C ● 12

D ● 16

37 Provide the missing number.

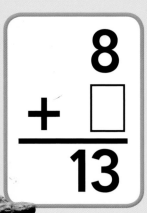

$$8 + \square = 13$$

A ● 6

B ● 3

C ● 4

D ● 5

38 Provide the missing number.

$$9 + \square = 14$$

A ● 5   C ● 6

B ● 4   D ● 7

39 Provide the missing number.

$$7 + \boxed{} = 12$$

A ● 3   C ● 5

B ● 4   D ● 6

40 Provide the missing number.

$$\begin{array}{r} \boxed{} \\ +\ 9 \\ \hline 17 \end{array}$$

A ● 6

B ● 8

C ● 9

D ● 11

41 How many are left?

$$\begin{array}{r} 3 \\ -\ 1 \\ \hline \end{array}$$

A ⬤ 0 C ⬤ 2

B ⬤ 3 D ⬤ 1

42 How many are left?

$$4 - 2 = \underline{}$$

A ⬤ 2 C ⬤ 5

B ⬤ 3 D ⬤ 6

How many are left?

$$5 - 2 = \underline{}$$

A ● 2   C ● 4

B ● 1   D ● 3

How many are left?

$$\begin{array}{r} 7 \\ -\ 3 \\ \hline \end{array}$$

A ● 3   C ● 5

B ● 4   D ● 2

How many are left?

$$\begin{array}{r} 8 \\ -\ 6 \\ \hline \end{array}$$

A ⬤ 3   C ⬤ 2

B ⬤ 4   D ⬤ 1

How many are left?

6 − 5 = __

A ⬤ 2   C ⬤ 0

B ⬤ 3   D ⬤ 1

47 How many are left?

$$10 - 4 = \_\_$$

A ● 6   C ● 4

B ● 5   D ● 3

48 How many are left?

$$\begin{array}{r} 12 \\ -\ 7 \\ \hline \end{array}$$

A ● 6   C ● 3

B ● 4   D ● 5

49

How many are left?

$$\begin{array}{r} 11 \\ -\ 4 \\ \hline \end{array}$$

A ● 8   C ● 9

B ● 7   D ● 6

50

How many are left?

17 − 3 = __

A ● 14   C ● 15

B ● 17   D ● 16

How many are left?

$$16 - 12 = \underline{}$$

A ● 4   C ● 6

B ● 5   D ● 3

How many are left?

$$\begin{array}{r} 18 \\ -\ 8 \\ \hline \end{array}$$

A ● 9   C ● 8

B ● 12   D ● 10

53 Find the difference.

$$2 - 1$$

A ⬤ 0
B ⬤ 1
C ⬤ 2
D ⬤ 3

54 Find the difference.

$$4 - 3 = \rule{2cm}{0.4pt}$$

A ⬤ 2   C ⬤ 3

B ⬤ 1   D ⬤ 4

Find the difference.

$$5 - 2 = \underline{\hspace{2cm}}$$

A ● 3   C ● 2

B ● 1   D ● 4

Find the difference.

$$\begin{array}{r} 7 \\ -\ 4 \\ \hline \end{array}$$

A ● 2

B ● 5

C ● 3

D ● 4

Find the difference.

$$6 - 2$$

A ● 2
B ● 5
C ● 3
D ● 4

Find the difference.

$$9 - 5 = \underline{}$$

A ● 4
B ● 5
C ● 3
D ● 7

©2017 The National Wildlife Federation

59

Find the difference.

$$10 - 9 = \underline{}$$

A ● 3   C ● 2

B ● 4   D ● 1

60

Find the difference.

$$\begin{array}{r} 8 \\ -\ 3 \\ \hline \end{array}$$

A ● 6

B ● 5

C ● 7

D ● 4

61 Find the difference.

$$12 - 8$$

A ● 4
B ● 3
C ● 2
D ● 5

62 Find the difference.

$$15 - 5 = \underline{\quad}$$

A ● 20
C ● 10
B ● 12
D ● 5

Find the difference.

$$16 - 12 = \rule{2cm}{0.4pt}$$

A ● 4   C ● 6

B ● 3   D ● 2

Find the difference.

$$\begin{array}{r} 14 \\ -\ 9 \\ \hline \end{array}$$

A ● 6

B ● 5

C ● 3

D ● 7

65

Find the difference.

$$17 - 6$$

A ● 8

B ● 6

C ● 11

D ● 10

66

Find the difference.

$$15 - 8 = \rule{1.5cm}{0.4pt}$$

A ● 6   C ● 8

B ● 5   D ● 7

67

Find the difference.

$$19 - 19 = \underline{\hspace{2cm}}$$

A ● 0   C ● 2

B ● 1   D ● 9

68

Find the difference.

$$\begin{array}{r} 13 \\ -7 \\ \hline \end{array}$$

A ● 4

B ● 6

C ● 8

D ● 7

69. Provide the missing number.

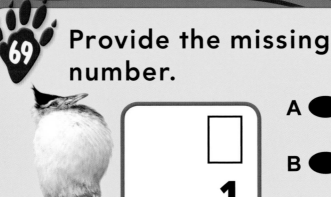

$$\square - 1 \over 4$$

- A ● 5
- B ● 6
- C ● 3
- D ● 7

70. Provide the missing number.

$$3 - \square = 1$$

- A ● 0
- B ● 1
- C ● 2
- D ● 4

71 Provide the missing number.

$$\boxed{} - 5 = 3$$

A ⬤ 5   C ⬤ 10

B ⬤ 7   D ⬤ 8

72 Provide the missing number.

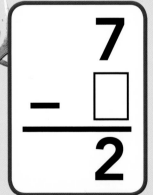

$$\begin{array}{r} 7 \\ - \ \boxed{} \\ \hline 2 \end{array}$$

A ⬤ 4

B ⬤ 5

C ⬤ 7

D ⬤ 6

73 Provide the missing number.

$$10 - \boxed{} \over 4$$

A ● 6

B ● 16

C ● 4

D ● 15

74 Provide the missing number.

$$\boxed{} - 2 = 9$$

A ● 7   C ● 12

B ● 8   D ● 11

Provide the missing number.

$$9 - \boxed{} = 0$$

A ● 7   C ● 9

B ● 11   D ● 0

Provide the missing number.

$$\begin{array}{r} \boxed{} \\ -\ 11 \\ \hline 3 \end{array}$$

A ● 14

B ● 18

C ● 19

D ● 4

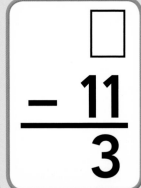

77 Provide the missing number.

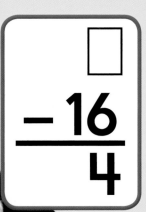

$$\begin{array}{r} \boxed{} \\ -\ 16 \\ \hline 4 \end{array}$$

A ● 18

B ● 20

C ● 17

D ● 19

78 Provide the missing number.

$$18 - \boxed{} = 15$$

A ● 0   C ● 3

B ● 1   D ● 2

Answer Key

1. B	21. C	41. C	61. A
2. D	22. A	42. A	62. C
3. A	23. D	43. D	63. A
4. B	24. A	44. B	64. B
5. D	25. B	45. C	65. C
6. A	26. C	46. D	66. D
7. C	27. A	47. A	67. A
8. B	28. D	48. D	68. B
9. D	29. C	49. B	69. A
10. D	30. B	50. A	70. C
11. A	31. A	51. A	71. D
12. A	32. C	52. D	72. B
13. B	33. D	53. B	73. A
14. A	34. A	54. B	74. D
15. D	35. B	55. A	75. C
16. B	36. A	56. C	76. A
17. B	37. D	57. D	77. B
18. C	38. A	58. A	78. C
19. A	39. C	59. D	
20. D	40. B	60. B	